3 american popular piano
SKILLS

T0080989

Created by
Dr. Scott McBride Smith

Series Composer
Christopher Norton

Editor
Dr. Scott McBride Smith

Associate Editor
Clarke MacIntosh

Book Design & Engraving
Andrew Jones

Cover Design
Wagner Design

Introduction

Everyone agrees that Tiger Woods is one of the greatest golfers of all time. Some even think he is the best ever! He won the 1997 Masters Tournament when he was 21 years old, the youngest winner in history. He was also the youngest golfer to complete a career *Grand Slam*, winning all four major championships by the age of 25.

How did he do it? Let's see what he says.

> *From early childhood I dreamed of being the world's best golfer. I worked hard and applied my family's values to everything I did. Integrity, honesty, discipline, responsiblity and fun; I learned these values at home and in school, each one pushing me further toward my dream.*

> Eldrick (Tiger) Woods
> Letter from Tiger, Tiger Woods Foundation Website
> http://www.twfound.org

> *The best way to achieve [a] goal is through sound fundamentals.*

> Tiger Woods
> *Golf Digest*, November 1998

What's your dream? Do you want to be one of the world's best musicians? play piano for your own enjoyment? or entertain your friends and family? No matter which, Tiger is right. Hard work, responsibility – and fun! – will be the keystones to your success.

In golf, the term "fundamentals" covers many things. In piano playing, we can break it down into three broad groupings.

- **Technic.** This is the ability to readily make the motions that create beautiful sounds. Dynamic control, tonal evenness and variety, and speed would fall into this category.

- **Sightreading.** You might also call these "quick learning" skills. Seeing patterns, noticing details, and playing without stopping – right away.

- **Listening.** This is perhaps the most important of all! If you can't hear the sounds of a piece in your mind before you play, you will never do a good job performing it. Psychologists call this "audiation".

Do you think practicing basic skills is boring? Get over it!

Your playing will never be as good or as enjoyable as you want it to be if your basic skills are not excellent. Every athlete – including Tiger – spends time on drills, exercises and warm-ups outside of the game. Pianists should, too. When your piano fundamentals become strong, you will learn everything more easily and perform more confidently.

This book is designed to help, but it won't work if you don't! Practice carefully and frequently. Spend some time every day on your basic skills and, who knows ... you may become the Tiger Woods of the piano.

Library and Archives Canada Cataloguing in Publication

Smith, Scott McBride

American popular piano [music] : skills / created by Scott McBride Smith ;
series composer, Christopher Norton ;
editor, Scott McBride Smith ; associate editor, Clarke MacIntosh.

To be complete in 11 volumes.
Publisher's nos.: APP S-00 (level P); APP S-01 (level 1); APP S-02 (level 2).
Contents: Preparatory level -- Level 1 -- Level 2.
Miscellaneous information: The series is organized in 11 levels, from preparatory to level 10, each including a repertoire album, an etudes album, a skills book, a "technic" book, and an instrumental backings compact disc.

ISBN 978-1-897379-22-6 (preparatory level).--ISBN 978-1-897379-23-3 (level 1).--
ISBN 978-1-897379-24-0 (level 2).--ISBN 978-1-897379-25-7 (level 3).--
ISBN 978-1-897379-26-4 (level 4).--ISBN 978-1-897379-27-1 (level 5)

1. Piano--Studies and exercises. 2. Piano--Studies and exercises--Juvenile.
I. Norton, Christopher, 1953- II. MacIntosh, S. Clarke, 1959- III. Title.

LEVEL ③ SKILLS
Table of Contents

2

Unit One - Module One

A. Technic

Set weekly practice schedule as assigned by your teacher. For directions, see *How to Use This Book* on page 50.

1) Triads (pages 44-45)

No.(s) _____ ;

M.M. ♩ = _____ ;

key(s): C G D

2) Arpeggios (pages 46-47)

No.(s) _____ ;

M.M. ♩ = _____ ;

key(s): C G

3) Drills (pages 48-49)

No.(s) _____ ;

M.M. ♩ = _____ ;

key(s): C G

4) Scales (pages 42-43)

No.(s) _____ ; M.M. ♩ = _____ ; key(s): C G D

Articulation: *legato   staccato   portato*

Dynamic: *f   p   mf   mp   ff   pp*

Dynamic Variant

< to top,   > to bottom

Rhythmic Variant

For *Basic* patterns   For *Complementary* patterns

B. Prepared Sightreading Piece

Play at least three times each week. Keep a steady beat.

For directions, see *How to Use This Book* on page 50.

C. Aural Skills - Rhythmic   For directions, see *How to Use This Book* on page 50.

1) Look at Exercises 2a, 2b, and 2c below. Fill in this chart, identifying which beats have rests. The first two have been done for you.

	m. 1	m. 2	m. 3	m. 4
Ex. 2a	none	1 - 2 - 3 - 4		
Ex. 2b				
Ex. 2c				

2) Clap each exercise with the backing track to *Lapping It Up* while counting out loud. Whisper and mime-clap (clap silently) the rests; clap and say the accented notes louder. Repeat until the end of the backing track.

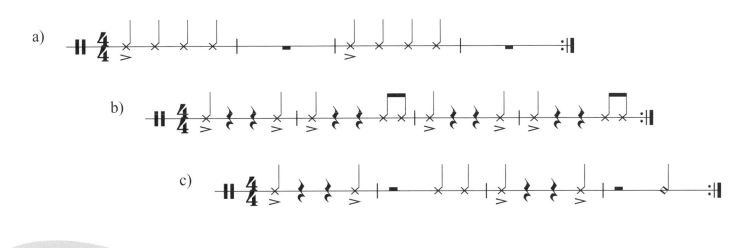

D. Aural Skills - Pitch   For directions, see *How to Use This Book* on page 50.

1) a) Label each triad with its letter name and chord type. Use a capital 'M' for major and a small 'm' for minor.

b) Play both triads. Now sing the scale degrees from each triad in the following order:

i)   4-6-1 5-3-1
ii) 6-4-1 3-5-1
iii) 1-6-4 1-5-3

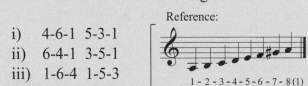

2) Sing and play the phrase simultaneously. Repeat, but don't play the last two notes – just sing them. Finally, just sing the entire phrase. What measures suggest an a minor triad? d minor? Label them. If you're not sure, try the two triads (from Ex.1, above) with your left hand while singing the phrase.

Unit One - Module Two

A. Technic

Set weekly practice schedule as assigned by your teacher. For directions, see *How to Use This Book* on page 50.

1) Triads (pages 44-45)

No.(s) _____ ;

M.M. ♩ = _____ ;

key(s): C G D

2) Arpeggios (pages 46-47)

No.(s) _____ ;

M.M. ♩ = _____ ;

key(s): C G

3) Drills (pages 48-49)

No.(s) _____ ;

M.M. ♩ = _____ ;

key(s): C G

4) Scales (pages 42-43)

No.(s) _____ ; M.M. ♩ = _____ ; key(s): C G D

Articulation: *legato   staccato   portato*

Dynamic: ***f   p   mf   mp   ff   pp***

Dynamic Variant

＞ to top,   ＜ to bottom

Rhythmic Variant

For *Basic* patterns   For *Complementary* patterns

B. Prepared Sightreading Piece

Play at least three times each week. Keep a steady beat.

For directions, see *How to Use This Book* on page 50.

C. Aural Skills - Rhythmic   For directions, see *How to Use This Book* on page 50.

1) Look at Exercises 2a, 2b, and 2c below. Fill in this chart, identifying which beats have rests. The first two have been done for you.

	m. 1	m. 2	m. 3	m. 4
Ex. 2a	**none**	**none**		
Ex. 2b				
Ex. 2c				

2) Clap each exercise with the backing track to *Jamaican Market* while counting out loud. Whisper and mime-clap (clap silently) the rests; clap and say the accented notes louder. Repeat until the end of the backing track.

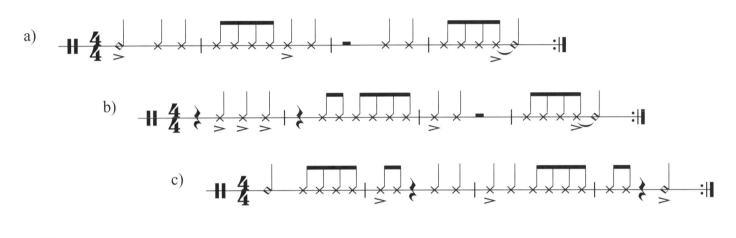

D. Aural Skills - Pitch   For directions, see *How to Use This Book* on page 50.

1) a) Label each triad with its letter name and chord type. Use a capital 'M' for major and a small 'm' for minor.

b) Play both triads. Now sing the scale degrees from each triad in the following order:

i)   5-7-2   1-3-5
ii) 7-2-5   5-3-1
iii) 2-5-7   3-5-1

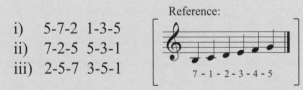

2) Sing and play the phrase simultaneously. Repeat, but don't play the last two notes – just sing them. Finally, just sing the entire phrase. What measures suggest a C major triad? G major? Label them.

Unit One - Module Three

A. Technic

Set weekly practice schedule as assigned by your teacher. For directions, see *How to Use This Book* on page 50.

1) Triads (pages 44-45)

No.(s) _____ ;

M.M. ♩ = _____ ;

key(s): C G D

2) Arpeggios (pages 46-47)

No.(s) _____ ;

M.M. ♩ = _____ ;

key(s): C G

3) Drills (pages 48-49)

No.(s) _____ ;

M.M. ♩ = _____ ;

key(s): C G

4) Scales (pages 42-43)

No.(s) _____ ; M.M. ♩ = _____ ; key(s): C G D

Articulation: *legato   staccato   portato*

Dynamic: *f   p   mf   mp   ff   pp*

Dynamic Variant

left hand *p* — right hand *f*

Rhythmic Variant

For *Basic* patterns   For *Complementary* patterns

B. Prepared Sightreading Piece

Play at least three times each week. Keep a steady beat.

For directions, see *How to Use This Book* on page 50.

C. Aural Skills - Rhythmic
For directions, see *How to Use This Book* on page 50.

1) Look at Exercises 2a, 2b, and 2c below. Fill in this chart, identifying which beats have rests. The first two have been done for you.

	m. 1	m. 2	m. 3	m. 4
Ex. 2a	none	1 - 2 - 3 - 4		
Ex. 2b				
Ex. 2c				

2) Clap each exercise with the backing track to *Tango of the Desert* while counting out loud. Whisper and mime-clap (clap silently) the rests; clap and say the accented notes louder. Repeat until the end of the backing track.

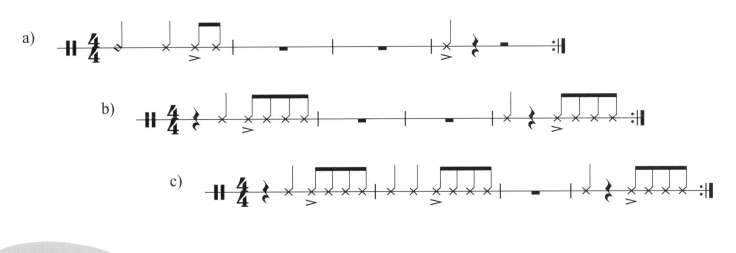

D. Aural Skills - Pitch
For directions, see *How to Use This Book* on page 50.

1) a) Label each triad with its letter name and chord type. Use a capital 'M' for major and a small 'm' for minor.

b) Play both triads. Now sing the scale degrees from each triad in the following order:

i)   5-3-1   5-7-2
ii)   3-1-5   2-7-5
iii)   1-5-3   7-2-5

Reference:

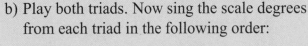

7 - 1 - 2 - 3 - 4 - 5

2) Sing and play the phrase simultaneously. Repeat, but don't play the last two notes – just sing them. Finally, just sing the entire phrase. What sections suggest a D major triad? A major? Label them.

Unit One - Module Four

A. Technic

Set weekly practice schedule as assigned by your teacher. For directions, see *How to Use This Book* on page 50.

1) Triads (pages 44-45)

No.(s) _____ ;

M.M. ♩ = _____ ;

key(s): C G D

2) Arpeggios (pages 46-47)

No.(s) _____ ;

M.M. ♩ = _____ ;

key(s): C G

3) Drills (pages 48-49)

No.(s) _____ ;

M.M. ♩ = _____ ;

key(s): C G

4) Scales (pages 42-43)

No.(s) _____ ; M.M. ♩ = _____ ; key(s): C G D

Articulation: *legato   staccato   portato*

Dynamic: *f   p   mf   mp   ff   pp*

Dynamic Variant

left hand *f* — right hand *p*

Rhythmic Variant

For *Basic* patterns   For *Complementary* patterns

B. Prepared Sightreading Piece

Play at least three times each week. Keep a steady beat.

For directions, see *How to Use This Book* on page 50.

C. Aural Skills - Rhythmic

For directions, see *How to Use This Book* on page 50.

1) Look at Exercises 2a, 2b, and 2c below. Fill in this chart, identifying which beats have rests. The first two have been done for you.

	m. 1	m. 2	m. 3	m. 4
Ex. 2a	none	none		
Ex. 2b				
Ex. 2c				

2) Clap each exercise with the backing track to *Country Boy* while counting out loud. Whisper and mime-clap (clap silently) the rests; clap and say the accented notes louder. Repeat until the end of the backing track.

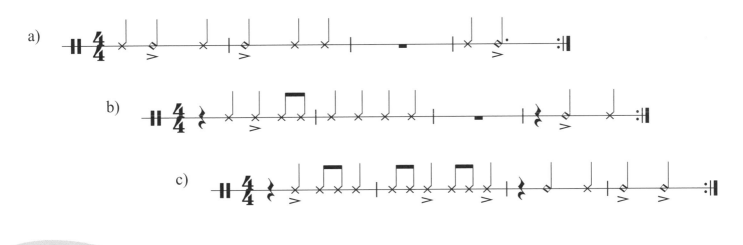

D. Aural Skills - Pitch

For directions, see *How to Use This Book* on page 50.

1) a) Label each triad with its letter name and chord type. Use a capital 'M' for major and a small 'm' for minor.

   b) Play both triads. Now sing the scale degrees from each triad in the following order:

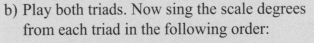

   i)   1-6-4   5-3-1
   ii) 1-4-6   5-3-1
   iii) 6-4-1   1-3-5

2) Sing and play the phrase simultaneously. Repeat, but don't play the last two notes – just sing them. Finally, just sing the entire phrase. What sections suggest an A major triad? D major? Label them.

Unit Two - Module One

A. Technic

Set weekly practice schedule as assigned by your teacher. For directions, see *How to Use This Book* on page 50.

1) Triads (pages 44-45)

No.(s) _____ ;

M.M. ♩ = _____ ;

key(s): D c g

2) Arpeggios (pages 46-47)

No.(s) _____ ;

M.M. ♩ = _____ ;

key(s): D c

3) Drills (pages 48-49)

No.(s) _____ ;

M.M. ♩ = _____ ;

key(s): D c

4) Scales (pages 42-43)

No.(s) _____ ; M.M. ♩ = _____ ; key(s): D c g

Articulation: *legato   staccato   portato*

Dynamic: *f   p   mf   mp   ff   pp*

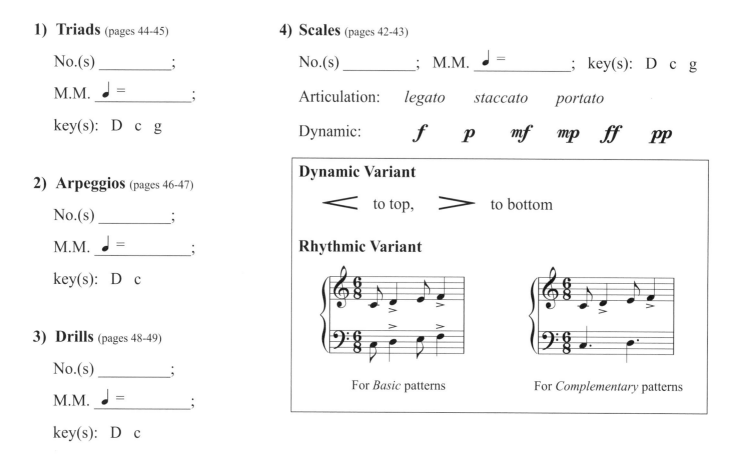

Dynamic Variant

< to top,   > to bottom

Rhythmic Variant

For *Basic* patterns   For *Complementary* patterns

B. Prepared Sightreading Piece

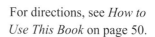
For directions, see *How to Use This Book* on page 50.

Play at least three times each week. Keep a steady beat.

C. Aural Skills - Rhythmic   For directions, see *How to Use This Book* on page 50.

1) Look at Exercises 2a, 2b, and 2c below. Fill in this chart, identifying which beats have rests. The first two have been done for you.

	m. 1	m. 2	m. 3	m. 4
Ex. 2a	**1 - & - 2**	**none**		
Ex. 2b				
Ex. 2c				

2) Clap each exercise with the backing track to *Tango of the Desert* while counting out loud. Whisper and mime-clap (clap silently) the rests; clap and say the accented notes louder. Repeat until the end of the backing track.

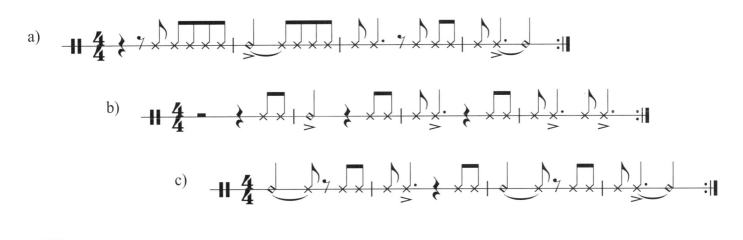

D. Aural Skills - Pitch   For directions, see *How to Use This Book* on page 50.

1) a) Label each triad with its letter name and chord type. Use a capital 'M' for major and a small 'm' for minor.

b) Play both triads. Now sing the scale degrees from each triad in the following order:

i)   5-7-2   5-3-1
ii) 2-5-7   1-5-3
iii) 7-5-2   3-5-1

Reference:

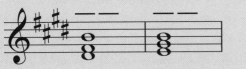

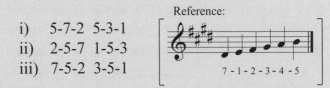

7 - 1 - 2 - 3 - 4 - 5

2) Sing and play the phrase simultaneously. Repeat, but don't play the last two notes – just sing them. Finally, just sing the entire phrase. What measures suggest an E major triad? B major? Label them.

E M

4

Unit Two - Module Two

A. Technic

Set weekly practice schedule as assigned by your teacher. For directions, see *How to Use This Book* on page 50.

1) Triads (pages 44-45)

No.(s) _____;

M.M. ♩ = _____;

key(s): D c g

2) Arpeggios (pages 46-47)

No.(s) _____;

M.M. ♩ = _____;

key(s): D c

3) Drills (pages 48-49)

No.(s) _____;

M.M. ♩ = _____;

key(s): D c

4) Scales (pages 42-43)

No.(s) _____; M.M. ♩ = _____; key(s): D c g

Articulation: *legato staccato portato*

Dynamic: *f p mf mp ff pp*

Dynamic Variant

> to top, < to bottom

Rhythmic Variant

For *Basic* patterns   For *Complementary* patterns

B. Prepared Sightreading Piece

For directions, see *How to Use This Book* on page 50.

Play at least three times each week. Keep a steady beat.

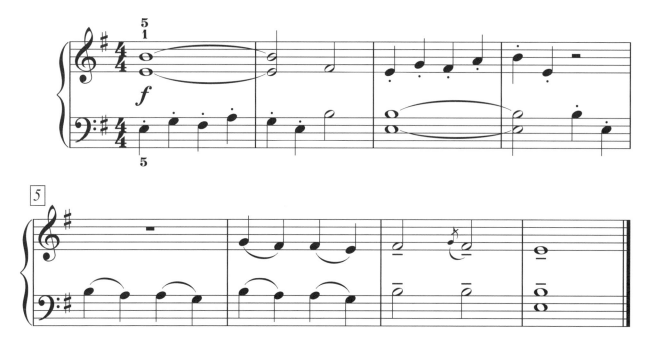

© Novus Via Music Group Inc. 2010. All rights reserved.

C. Aural Skills - Rhythmic
For directions, see *How to Use This Book* on page 50.

1) Look at Exercises 2a, 2b, and 2c below. Fill in this chart, identifying which beats have rests. The first two have been done for you.

	m. 1	m. 2	m. 3	m. 4
Ex. 2a	none	3 - &		
Ex. 2b				
Ex. 2c				

2) Clap each exercise with the backing track to *Jamaican Market* while counting out loud. Whisper and mime-clap (clap silently) the rests; clap and say the accented notes louder. Repeat until the end of the backing track.

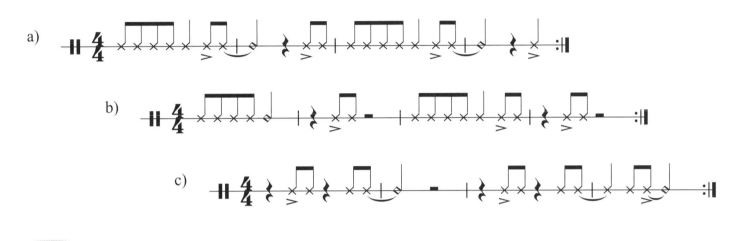

D. Aural Skills - Pitch
For directions, see *How to Use This Book* on page 50.

1) a) Label each triad with its letter name and chord type. Use a capital 'M' for major and a small 'm' for minor.

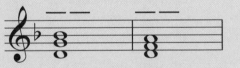

   b) Play both triads. Now sing the scale degrees from each triad in the following order:

   i)   6-4-1 5-3-1
   ii) 1-6-4 3-5-1
   iii) 4-6-1 1-3-5

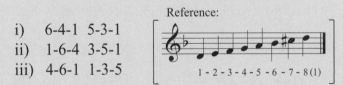

   Reference:

   1 - 2 - 3 - 4 - 5 - 6 - 7 - 8 (1)

2) Sing and play the phrase simultaneously. Repeat, but don't play the last two notes – just sing them. Finally, just sing the entire phrase. What measures suggest a d minor triad? g minor? Label them.

D m

4

Unit Two - Module Three

A. Technic

Set weekly practice schedule as assigned by your teacher. For directions, see *How to Use This Book* on page 50.

1) Triads (pages 44-45)

No.(s) _____ ;

M.M. ♩ = _____ ;

key(s): D c g

2) Arpeggios (pages 46-47)

No.(s) _____ ;

M.M. ♩ = _____ ;

key(s): D c

3) Drills (pages 48-49)

No.(s) _____ ;

M.M. ♩ = _____ ;

key(s): D c

4) Scales (pages 42-43)

No.(s) _____ ; M.M. ♩ = _____ ; key(s): D c g

Articulation: *legato   staccato   portato*

Dynamic: **f   p   mf   mp   ff   pp**

Dynamic Variant

left hand **p** — right hand **f**

Rhythmic Variant

For *Basic* patterns   For *Complementary* patterns

B. Prepared Sightreading Piece

Play at least three times each week. Keep a steady beat.

For directions, see *How to Use This Book* on page 50.

C. Aural Skills - Rhythmic   For directions, see *How to Use This Book* on page 50.

1) Look at Exercises 2a, 2b, and 2c below. Fill in this chart, identifying which beats have rests. The first two have been done for you.

	m. 1	m. 2	m. 3	m. 4
Ex. 2a	none	2 - & - 3 - &		
Ex. 2b				
Ex. 2c				

2) Clap each exercise with the backing track to *Tango of the Desert* while counting out loud. Whisper and mime-clap (clap silently) the rests; clap and say the accented notes louder. Repeat until the end of the backing track.

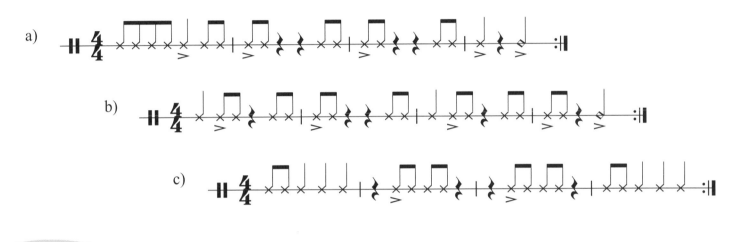

a)

b)

c)

D. Aural Skills - Pitch   For directions, see *How to Use This Book* on page 50.

1) a) Label each triad with its letter name and chord type. Use a capital 'M' for major and a small 'm' for minor.

b) Play both triads. Now sing the scale degrees from each triad in the following order:

   i)   2-5-7   5-3-1
   ii) 5-7-2   5-1-3
   iii) 7-5-2   1-5-3

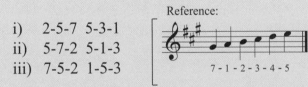

Reference:

7 - 1 - 2 - 3 - 4 - 5

2) Sing and play the phrase simultaneously. Repeat, but don't play the last two notes – just sing them. Finally, just sing the entire phrase. What measures suggest an A major triad? E major? Label them.

A M

6

Unit Two - Module Four

A. Technic

Set weekly practice schedule as assigned by your teacher. For directions, see *How to Use This Book* on page 50.

1) Triads (pages 44-45)

No.(s) _____;

M.M. ♩ = _____;

key(s): D c g

2) Arpeggios (pages 46-47)

No.(s) _____;

M.M. ♩ = _____;

key(s): D c

3) Drills (pages 48-49)

No.(s) _____;

M.M. ♩ = _____;

key(s): D c

4) Scales (pages 42-43)

No.(s) _____; M.M. ♩ = _____; key(s): D c g

Articulation: *legato* *staccato* *portato*

Dynamic: ***f*** ***p*** ***mf*** ***mp*** ***ff*** ***pp***

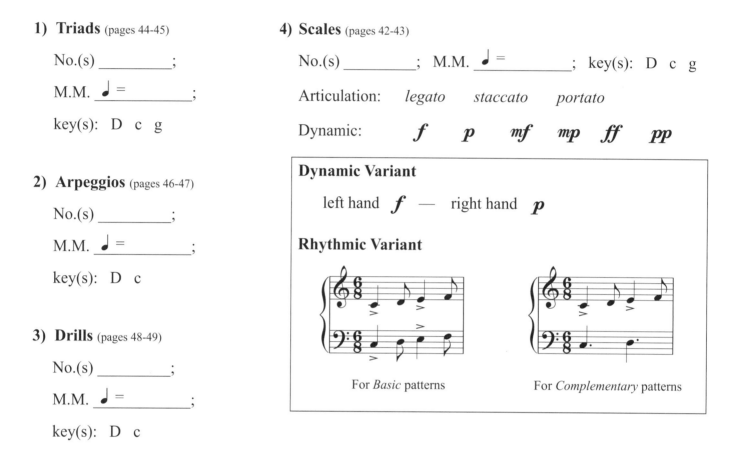

Dynamic Variant

left hand ***f*** — right hand ***p***

Rhythmic Variant

For *Basic* patterns   For *Complementary* patterns

B. Prepared Sightreading Piece

Play at least three times each week. Keep a steady beat.

For directions, see *How to Use This Book* on page 50.

C. Aural Skills - Rhythmic

For directions, see *How to Use This Book* on page 50.

1) Look at Exercises 2a, 2b, and 2c below. Fill in this chart, identifying which beats have rests. The first two have been done for you.

	m. 1	m. 2	m. 3	m. 4
Ex. 2a	**2**	**1 - &**		
Ex. 2b				
Ex. 2c				

2) Clap each exercise with the backing track to *Lapping It Up* while counting out loud. Whisper and mime-clap (clap silently) the rests; clap and say the accented notes louder. Repeat until the end of the backing track.

a) 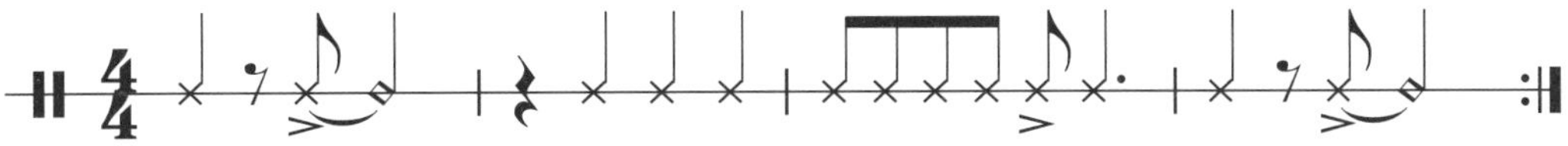

b) 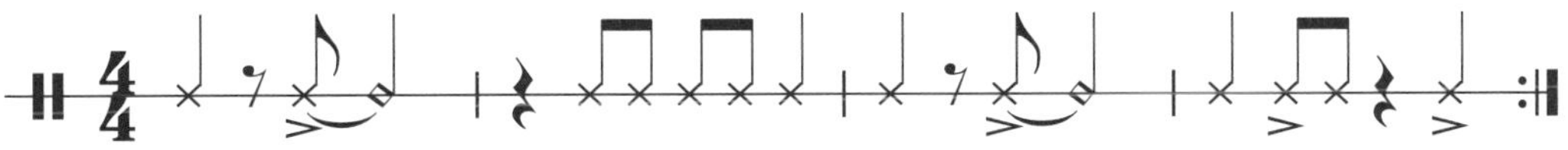

c) 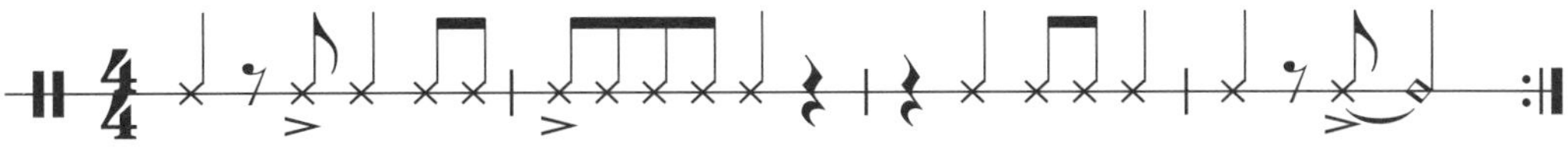

D. Aural Skills - Pitch

For directions, see *How to Use This Book* on page 50.

1) a) Label each triad with its letter name and chord type. Use a capital 'M' for major and a small 'm' for minor.

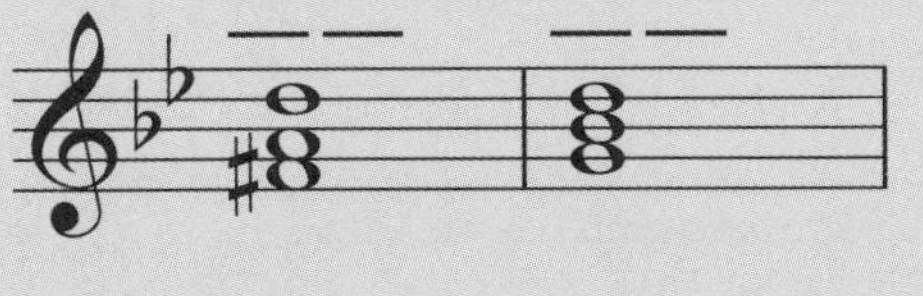

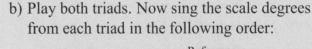

b) Play both triads. Now sing the scale degrees from each triad in the following order:

i) 7-5-2 1-5-3
ii) 5-7-2 5-1-3
iii) 2-5-7 3-5-1

Reference:

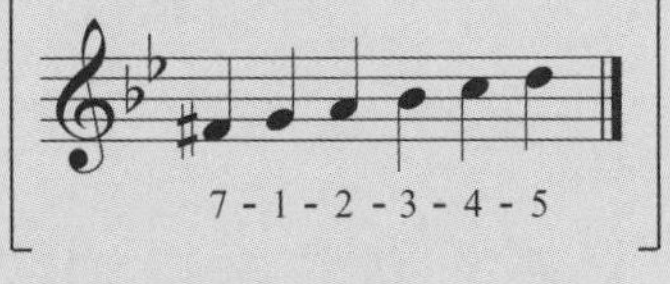

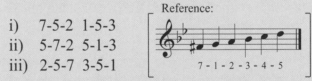

2) Sing and play the phrase simultaneously. Repeat, but don't play the last two notes – just sing them. Finally, just sing the entire phrase. What sections suggest a g minor triad? D major? Label them.

Unit Three - Module One

A. Technic

Set weekly practice schedule as assigned by your teacher. For directions, see *How to Use This Book* on page 50.

1) Triads (pages 44-45)

No.(s) _____;

M.M. ♩ = _____;

key(s): g A E

2) Arpeggios (pages 46-47)

No.(s) _____;

M.M. ♩ = _____;

key(s): g A

3) Drills (pages 48-49)

No.(s) _____;

M.M. ♩ = _____;

key(s): g A

4) Scales (pages 42-43)

No.(s) _____; M.M. ♩ = _____; key(s): g A E

Articulation: *legato   staccato   portato*

Dynamic: ***f***   ***p***   ***mf***   ***mp***   ***ff***   ***pp***

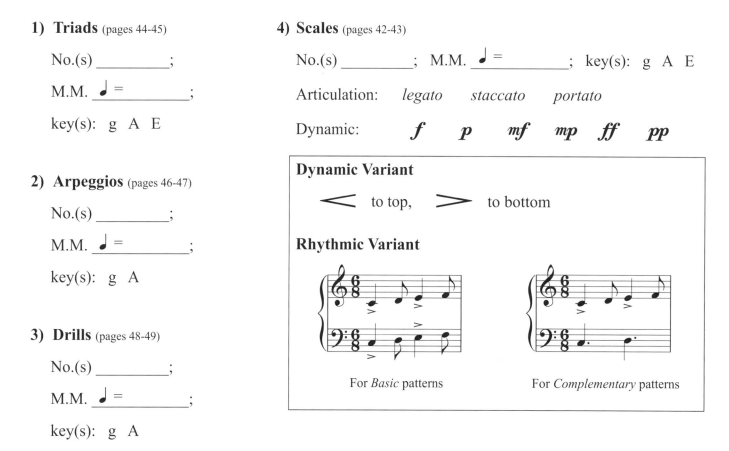

Dynamic Variant

< to top,   > to bottom

Rhythmic Variant

For *Basic* patterns   For *Complementary* patterns

B. Prepared Sightreading Piece

Play at least three times each week. Keep a steady beat.

For directions, see *How to Use This Book* on page 50.

C. Aural Skills - Rhythmic   For directions, see *How to Use This Book* on page 50.

1) Look at Exercises 2a, 2b, and 2c below. Fill in this chart, identifying which beats have rests. The first two have been done for you.

	m. 1	m. 2	m. 3	m. 4
Ex. 2a	none	2 - & - 3 - &		
Ex. 2b				
Ex. 2c				

2) Clap each exercise with the backing track to *Country Boy* while counting out loud. Whisper and mime-clap (clap silently) the rests; clap and say the accented notes louder. Repeat until the end of the backing track.

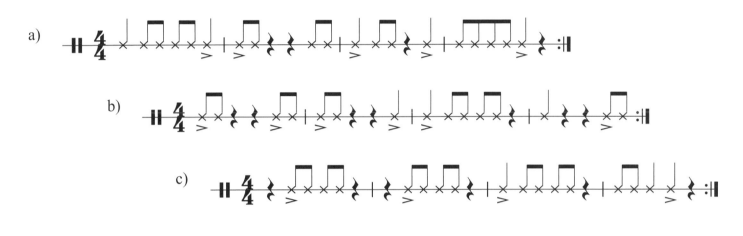

D. Aural Skills - Pitch   For directions, see *How to Use This Book* on page 50.

1) a) Label each triad with its letter name and chord type. Use a capital 'M' for major and a small 'm' for minor.

b) Play both triads. Now sing the scale degrees from each triad in the following order:

i)   6-1-4   5-1-3
ii) 4-1-6   3-5-1
iii) 1-4-6   1-5-3

Reference:

1 - 2 - 3 - 4 - 5 - 6 - 7 - 8 (1)

2) Sing and play the phrase simultaneously. Repeat, but don't play the last two notes – just sing them. Finally, just sing the entire phrase. What sections suggest an a minor triad? d minor? Label them.

Unit Three - Module Two

A. Technic

Set weekly practice schedule as assigned by your teacher. For directions, see *How to Use This Book* on page 50.

1) Triads (pages 44-45)

No.(s) _____ ;

M.M. ♩ = _____ ;

key(s): g A E

2) Arpeggios (pages 46-47)

No.(s) _____ ;

M.M. ♩ = _____ ;

key(s): g A

3) Drills (pages 48-49)

No.(s) _____ ;

M.M. ♩ = _____ ;

key(s): g A

4) Scales (pages 42-43)

No.(s) _____ ; M.M. ♩ = _____ ; key(s): g A E

Articulation: *legato   staccato   portato*

Dynamic: *f   p   mf   mp   ff   pp*

Dynamic Variant

> to top,   < to bottom

Rhythmic Variant

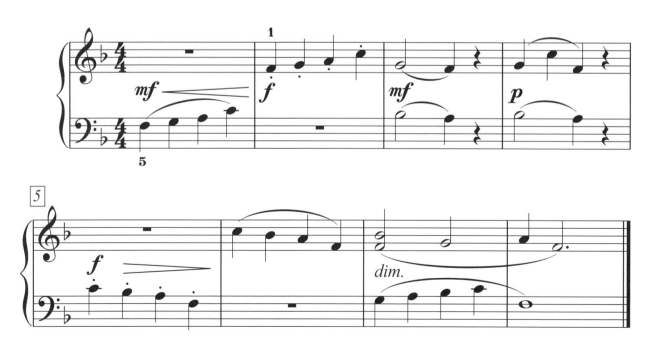

For *Basic* patterns   For *Complementary* patterns

B. Prepared Sightreading Piece

Play at least three times each week. Keep a steady beat.

For directions, see *How to Use This Book* on page 50.

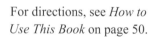

C. Aural Skills - Rhythmic   For directions, see *How to Use This Book* on page 50.

1) Look at Exercises 2a, 2b, and 2c below. Fill in this chart, identifying which beats have rests. The first two have been done for you.

	m. 1	m. 2	m. 3	m. 4
Ex. 2a	none	2 - &		
Ex. 2b				
Ex. 2c				

2) Clap each exercise with the backing track to *Lapping It Up* while counting out loud. Whisper and mime-clap (clap silently) the rests; clap and say the accented notes louder. Repeat until the end of the backing track.

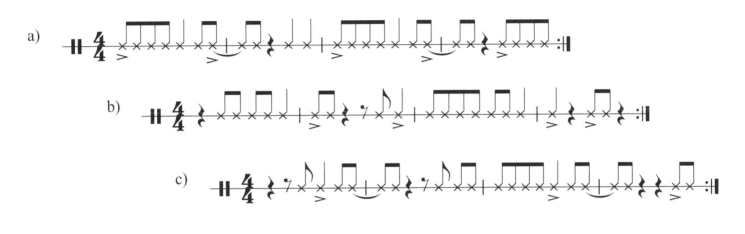

D. Aural Skills - Pitch   For directions, see *How to Use This Book* on page 50.

1) a) Label each triad with its letter name and chord type. Use a capital 'M' for major and a small 'm' for minor.

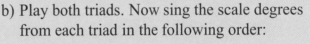

b) Play both triads. Now sing the scale degrees from each triad in the following order:

i)   2-5-7 3-8-5
ii) 5-7-2 8-5-3
iii) 7-2-5 5-8-3

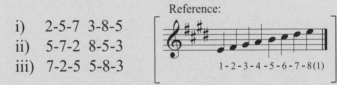

2) Sing and play the phrase simultaneously. Repeat, but don't play the last two notes – just sing them. Finally, just sing the entire phrase. What sections suggest an E major triad? B major? Label them.

Unit Three - Module Three

A. Technic

Set weekly practice schedule as assigned by your teacher. For directions, see *How to Use This Book* on page 50.

1) Triads (pages 44-45)

No.(s) _____ ;

M.M. ♩ = _____ ;

key(s): g A E

2) Arpeggios (pages 46-47)

No.(s) _____ ;

M.M. ♩ = _____ ;

key(s): g A

3) Drills (pages 48-49)

No.(s) _____ ;

M.M. ♩ = _____ ;

key(s): g A

4) Scales (pages 42-43)

No.(s) _____ ; M.M. ♩ = _____ ; key(s): g A E

Articulation: *legato*   *staccato*   *portato*

Dynamic: *f* *p* *mf* *mp* *ff* *pp*

Dynamic Variant

left hand *p* — right hand *f*

Rhythmic Variant

For *Basic* patterns   For *Complementary* patterns

B. Prepared Sightreading Piece

Play at least three times each week. Keep a steady beat.

For directions, see *How to Use This Book* on page 50.

C. Aural Skills - Rhythmic   For directions, see *How to Use This Book* on page 50.

1) Look at Exercises 2a, 2b, and 2c below. Fill in this chart, identifying which beats have rests. The first two have been done for you.

	m. 1	m. 2	m. 3	m. 4
Ex. 2a	**none**	**3 - & - 4**		
Ex. 2b				
Ex. 2c				

2) Clap each exercise with the backing track to *Tango of the Desert* while counting out loud. Whisper and mime-clap (clap silently) the rests; clap and say the accented notes louder. Repeat until the end of the backing track.

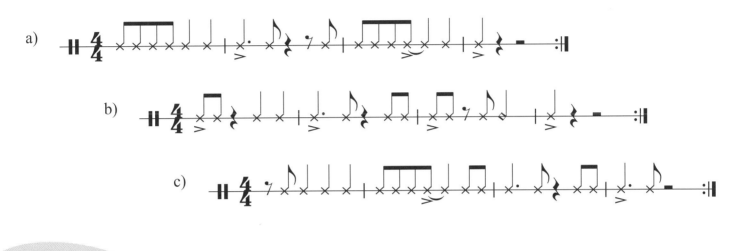

D. Aural Skills - Pitch   For directions, see *How to Use This Book* on page 50.

1) a) Label each triad with its letter name and chord type. Use a capital 'M' for major and a small 'm' for minor.

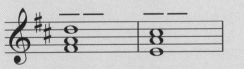

b) Play both triads. Now sing the scale degrees from each triad in the following order:

i)   8-3-5 2-7-5
ii) 3-5-8 5-7-2
iii) 5-3-8 7-2-5

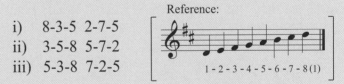

Reference:

1 - 2 - 3 - 4 - 5 - 6 - 7 - 8 (1)

2) Sing and play the phrase simultaneously. Repeat, but don't play the last two notes – just sing them. Finally, just sing the entire phrase. What measures suggest a D major triad? A major? Label them.

Unit Three - Module Four

A. Technic

Set weekly practice schedule as assigned by your teacher. For directions, see *How to Use This Book* on page 50.

1) Triads (pages 44-45)

No.(s) _____;

M.M. ♩ = _____;

key(s): g A E

2) Arpeggios (pages 46-47)

No.(s) _____;

M.M. ♩ = _____;

key(s): g A

3) Drills (pages 48-49)

No.(s) _____;

M.M. ♩ = _____;

key(s): g A

4) Scales (pages 42-43)

No.(s) _____; M.M. ♩ = _____; key(s): g A E

Articulation: *legato   staccato   portato*

Dynamic: *f*   *p*   *mf*   *mp*   *ff*   *pp*

Dynamic Variant

left hand *f* — right hand *p*

Rhythmic Variant

For *Basic* patterns   For *Complementary* patterns

B. Prepared Sightreading Piece

Play at least three times each week. Keep a steady beat.

For directions, see *How to Use This Book* on page 50.

C. Aural Skills - Rhythmic   For directions, see *How to Use This Book* on page 50.

1) Look at Exercises 2a, 2b, and 2c below. Fill in this chart, identifying which beats have rests. The first two have been done for you.

	m. 1	m. 2	m. 3	m. 4
Ex. 2a	3 - & - 4 - &	none		
Ex. 2b				
Ex. 2c				

2) Clap each exercise with the backing track to *Lapping It Up* while counting out loud. Whisper and mime-clap (clap silently) the rests; clap and say the accented notes louder. Repeat until the end of the backing track.

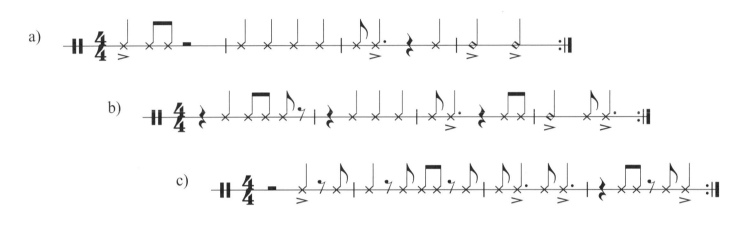

D. Aural Skills - Pitch   For directions, see *How to Use This Book* on page 50.

1) a) Label each triad with its letter name and chord type. Use a capital 'M' for major and a small 'm' for minor.

b) Play both triads. Now sing the scale degrees from each triad in the following order:

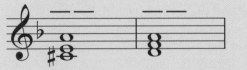

   i)   5-2-7 3-5-1
   ii) 7-5-2 1-5-3
   iii) 2-5-7 5-3-1

Reference:

7 - 1 - 2 - 3 - 4 - 5

2) Sing and play the phrase simultaneously. Repeat, but don't play the last two notes – just sing them. Finally, just sing the entire phrase. What sections suggest a d minor triad? A major? Label them.

Unit Four - Module One

A. Technic

Set weekly practice schedule as assigned by your teacher. For directions, see *How to Use This Book* on page 50.

1) Triads (pages 44-45)

No.(s) _____ ;

M.M. ♩ = _____ ;

key(s): E d a

2) Arpeggios (pages 46-47)

No.(s) _____ ;

M.M. ♩ = _____ ;

key(s): E d

3) Drills (pages 48-49)

No.(s) _____ ;

M.M. ♩ = _____ ;

key(s): E d

4) Scales (pages 42-43)

No.(s) _____ ; M.M. ♩ = _____ ; key(s): E d a

Articulation: *legato   staccato   portato*

Dynamic: ***f   p   mf   mp   ff   pp***

Dynamic Variant

< to top, > to bottom

Rhythmic Variant

For *Basic* patterns   For *Complementary* patterns

B. Prepared Sightreading Piece

Play at least three times each week. Keep a steady beat.

For directions, see *How to Use This Book* on page 50.

C. Aural Skills - Rhythmic

For directions, see *How to Use This Book* on page 50.

1) Look at Exercises 2a, 2b, and 2c below. Fill in this chart, identifying which beats have rests. The first two have been done for you.

	m. 1	m. 2	m. 3	m. 4
Ex. 2a	none	none		
Ex. 2b				
Ex. 2c				

2) Clap each exercise with the backing track to *Tango of the Desert* while counting out loud. Whisper and mime-clap (clap silently) the rests; clap and say the accented notes louder. Repeat until the end of the backing track.

a)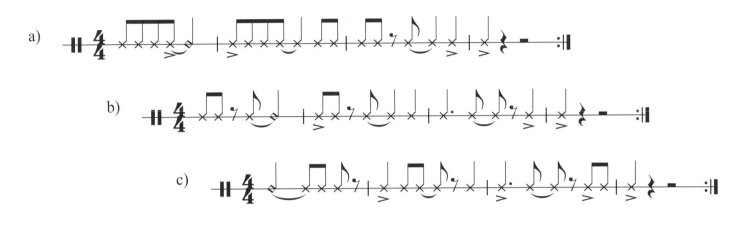

b)

c)

D. Aural Skills - Pitch

For directions, see *How to Use This Book* on page 50.

1) a) Label each triad with its letter name and chord type. Use a capital 'M' for major and a small 'm' for minor.

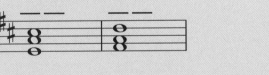

b) Play both triads. Now sing the scale degrees from each triad in the following order:

i)   2-5-7   3-5-8
ii) 5-7-2   5-8-3
iii) 7-2-5   8-5-3

Reference:

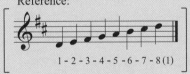

1 - 2 - 3 - 4 - 5 - 6 - 7 - 8 (1)

2) Sing and play the phrase simultaneously. Repeat, but don't play the last two notes – just sing them. Finally, just sing the entire phrase. What sections suggest a D major triad? A major? Label them.

D M

4

Unit Four - Module Two

A. Technic

Set weekly practice schedule as assigned by your teacher. For directions, see *How to Use This Book* on page 50.

1) Triads (pages 44-45)

No.(s) _____;

M.M. ♩ = _____;

key(s): E d a

2) Arpeggios (pages 46-47)

No.(s) _____;

M.M. ♩ = _____;

key(s): E d

3) Drills (pages 48-49)

No.(s) _____;

M.M. ♩ = _____;

key(s): E d

4) Scales (pages 42-43)

No.(s) _____; M.M. ♩ = _____; key(s): E d a

Articulation: *legato   staccato   portato*

Dynamic: ***f   p   mf   mp   ff   pp***

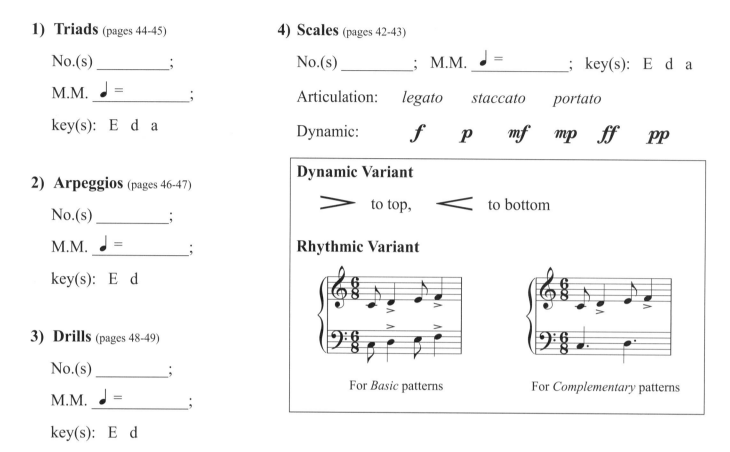

Dynamic Variant

> to top,   < to bottom

Rhythmic Variant

For *Basic* patterns   For *Complementary* patterns

B. Prepared Sightreading Piece

Play at least three times each week. Keep a steady beat.

For directions, see *How to Use This Book* on page 50.

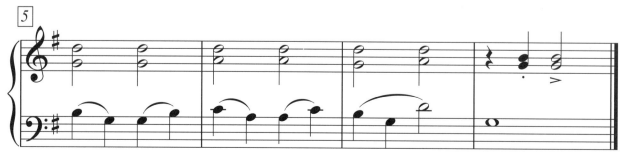

C. Aural Skills - Rhythmic   For directions, see *How to Use This Book* on page 50.

1) Look at Exercises 2a, 2b, and 2c below. Fill in this chart, identifying which beats have rests. The first two have been done for you.

	m. 1	m. 2	m. 3	m. 4
Ex. 2a	2, 3	2, 3 - & - 4 - &		
Ex. 2b				
Ex. 2c				

2) Clap each exercise with the backing track to *Jamaican Market* while counting out loud. Whisper and mime-clap (clap silently) the rests; clap and say the accented notes louder. Repeat until the end of the backing track.

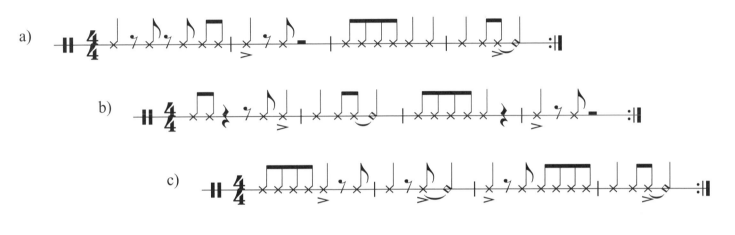

D. Aural Skills - Pitch   For directions, see *How to Use This Book* on page 50.

1) a) Label each triad with its letter name and chord type. Use a capital 'M' for major and a small 'm' for minor.

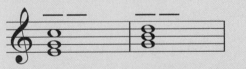

b) Play both triads. Now sing the scale degrees from each triad in the following order:

i)   3-1-5 5-2-7
ii) 1-5-3 2-5-7
iii) 3-5-1 7-5-2

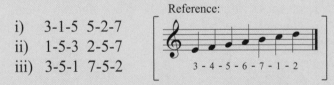

2) Sing and play the phrase simultaneously. Repeat, but don't play the last two notes – just sing them. Finally, just sing the entire phrase. What sections suggest a C major triad? G major? Label them.

Unit Four - Module Three

A. Technic

Set weekly practice schedule as assigned by your teacher. For directions, see *How to Use This Book* on page 50.

1) Triads (pages 44-45)

No.(s) _____ ;

M.M. ♩ = _____ ;

key(s): E d a

2) Arpeggios (pages 46-47)

No.(s) _____ ;

M.M. ♩ = _____ ;

key(s): E d

3) Drills (pages 48-49)

No.(s) _____ ;

M.M. ♩ = _____ ;

key(s): E d

4) Scales (pages 42-43)

No.(s) _____ ; M.M. ♩ = _____ ; key(s): E d a

Articulation: *legato*   *staccato*   *portato*

Dynamic: *f*   *p*   *mf*   *mp*   *ff*   *pp*

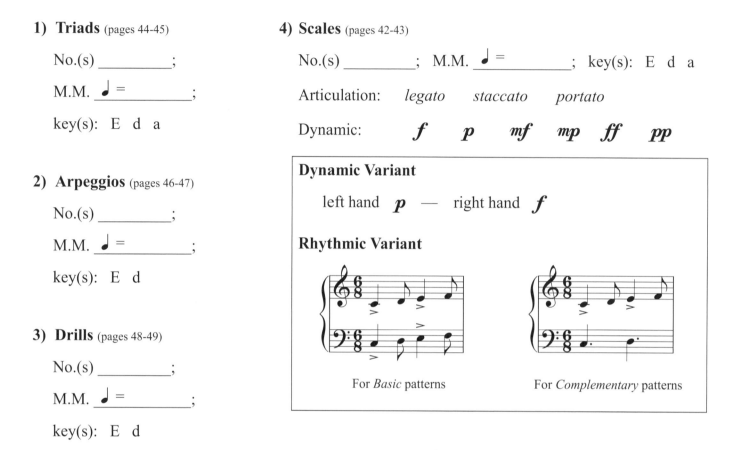

Dynamic Variant

left hand *p* — right hand *f*

Rhythmic Variant

For *Basic* patterns   For *Complementary* patterns

B. Prepared Sightreading Piece

Play at least three times each week. Keep a steady beat.

For directions, see *How to Use This Book* on page 50.

C. Aural Skills - Rhythmic

For directions, see *How to Use This Book* on page 50.

1) Look at Exercises 2a, 2b, and 2c below. Fill in this chart, identifying which beats have rests. The first two have been done for you.

	m. 1	m. 2	m. 3	m. 4
Ex. 2a	none	2		
Ex. 2b				
Ex. 2c				

2) Clap each exercise with the backing track to *Lapping It Up* while counting out loud. Whisper and mime-clap (clap silently) the rests; clap and say the accented notes louder. Repeat until the end of the backing track.

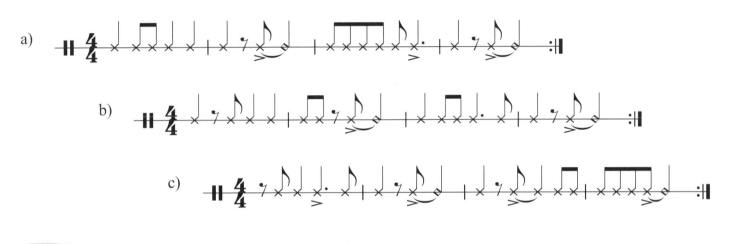

D. Aural Skills - Pitch

For directions, see *How to Use This Book* on page 50.

1) a) Label each triad with its letter name and chord type. Use a capital 'M' for major and a small 'm' for minor.

b) Play both triads. Now sing the scale degrees from each triad in the following order:

i) 6-8-4 3-8-5
ii) 8-4-6 8-5-3
iii) 4-8-6 5-3-8

Reference:

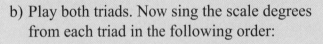

1 - 2 - 3 - 4 - 5 - 6 - 7 - 8 (1)

2) Sing and play the phrase simultaneously. Repeat, but don't play the last two notes – just sing them. Finally, just sing the entire phrase. What measures suggest an E major triad? A major? Label them.

Unit Four - Module Four

A. Technic

Set weekly practice schedule as assigned by your teacher. For directions, see *How to Use This Book* on page 50.

1) Triads (pages 44-45)

No.(s) _____ ;

M.M. ♩ = _____ ;

key(s): E d a

2) Arpeggios (pages 46-47)

No.(s) _____ ;

M.M. ♩ = _____ ;

key(s): E d

3) Drills (pages 48-49)

No.(s) _____ ;

M.M. ♩ = _____ ;

key(s): E d

4) Scales (pages 42-43)

No.(s) _____ ; M.M. ♩ = _____ ; key(s): E d a

Articulation: *legato   staccato   portato*

Dynamic: ***f   p   mf   mp   ff   pp***

Dynamic Variant

left hand ***f*** — right hand ***p***

Rhythmic Variant

For *Basic* patterns   For *Complementary* patterns

B. Prepared Sightreading Piece

Play at least three times each week. Keep a steady beat.

For directions, see *How to Use This Book* on page 50.

C. Aural Skills - Rhythmic   For directions, see *How to Use This Book* on page 50.

1) Look at Exercises 2a, 2b, and 2c below. Fill in this chart, identifying which beats have rests. The first two have been done for you.

	m. 1	m. 2	m. 3	m. 4
Ex. 2a	none	none		
Ex. 2b				
Ex. 2c				

2) Clap each exercise with the backing track to *Country Boy* while counting out loud. Whisper and mime-clap (clap silently) the rests; clap and say the accented notes louder. Repeat until the end of the backing track.

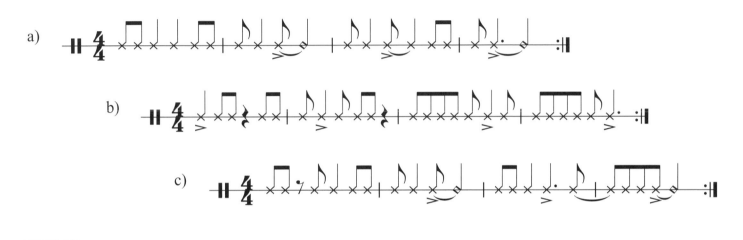

D. Aural Skills - Pitch   For directions, see *How to Use This Book* on page 50.

1) a) Label each triad with its letter name and chord type. Use a capital 'M' for major and a small 'm' for minor.

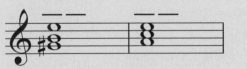

b) Play both triads. Now sing the scale degrees from each triad in the following order:

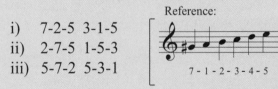

i)   7-2-5 3-1-5
ii) 2-7-5 1-5-3
iii) 5-7-2 5-3-1

Reference:
7 - 1 - 2 - 3 - 4 - 5

2) Sing and play the phrase simultaneously. Repeat, but don't play the last two notes – just sing them. Finally, just sing the entire phrase. What sections suggest an a minor triad? E major? Label them.

Unit 1 - Midterm

I. Technic   Grade ☐

A. Triads
No.(s) _____ ; key(s) _____ ; M.M. _____ ;

B. Arpeggios
No.(s) _____ ; key(s) _____ ; M.M. _____ ;

C. Drills
No.(s) _____ ; key(s) _____ ; M.M. _____ ;

D. Scales
No.(s) _____ ; key(s) _____ ; M.M. _____ ;

II. Sightreading   Grade ☐   Student may study for up to 15 seconds.

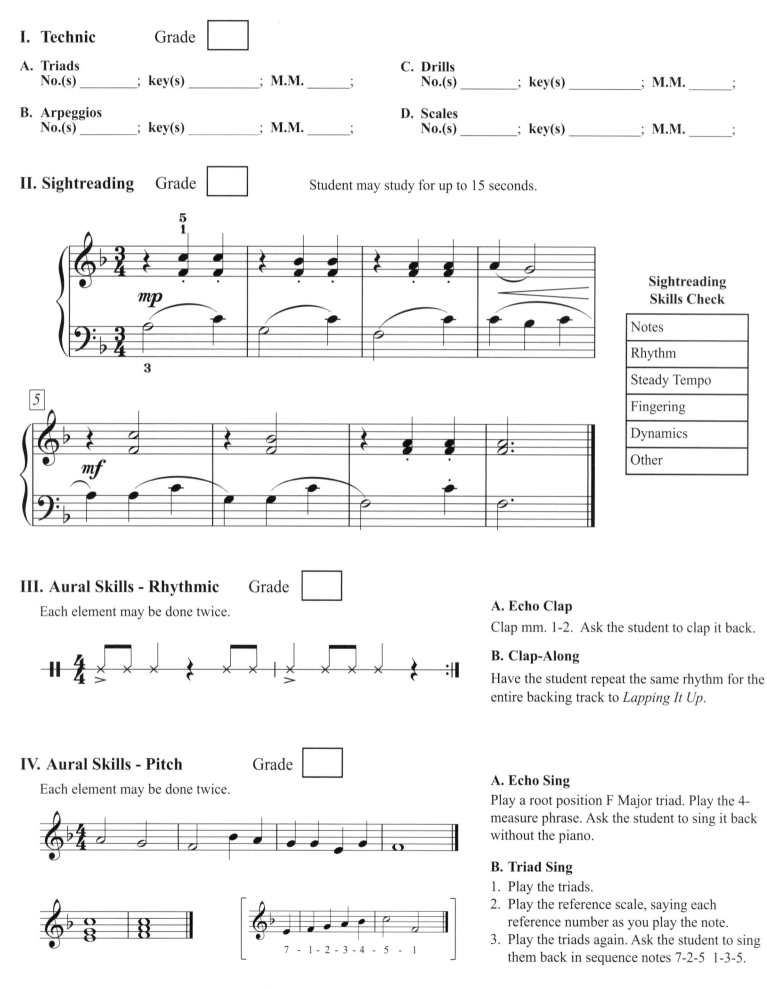

Sightreading Skills Check
Notes
Rhythm
Steady Tempo
Fingering
Dynamics
Other

III. Aural Skills - Rhythmic   Grade ☐

Each element may be done twice.

A. Echo Clap

Clap mm. 1-2. Ask the student to clap it back.

B. Clap-Along

Have the student repeat the same rhythm for the entire backing track to *Lapping It Up*.

IV. Aural Skills - Pitch   Grade ☐

Each element may be done twice.

A. Echo Sing

Play a root position F Major triad. Play the 4-measure phrase. Ask the student to sing it back without the piano.

B. Triad Sing

1. Play the triads.
2. Play the reference scale, saying each reference number as you play the note.
3. Play the triads again. Ask the student to sing them back in sequence notes 7-2-5 1-3-5.

Unit 1 - Final

I. Technic   Grade ⬚

A. Triads
No.(s) _____ ; key(s) _____ ; M.M. _____ ;

C. Drills
No.(s) _____ ; key(s) _____ ; M.M. _____ ;

B. Arpeggios
No.(s) _____ ; key(s) _____ ; M.M. _____ ;

D. Scales
No.(s) _____ ; key(s) _____ ; M.M. _____ ;

II. Sightreading   Grade ⬚   Student may study for up to 15 seconds.

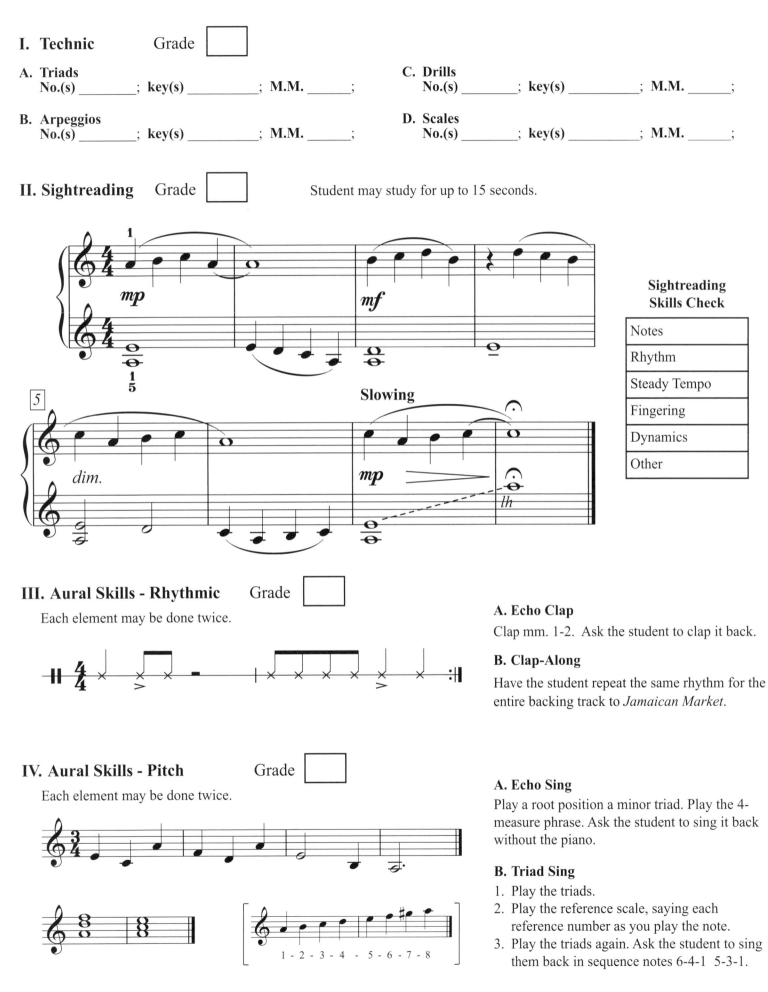

Sightreading Skills Check

Notes
Rhythm
Steady Tempo
Fingering
Dynamics
Other

III. Aural Skills - Rhythmic   Grade ⬚

Each element may be done twice.

A. Echo Clap
Clap mm. 1-2. Ask the student to clap it back.

B. Clap-Along
Have the student repeat the same rhythm for the entire backing track to *Jamaican Market*.

IV. Aural Skills - Pitch   Grade ⬚

Each element may be done twice.

A. Echo Sing
Play a root position a minor triad. Play the 4-measure phrase. Ask the student to sing it back without the piano.

B. Triad Sing
1. Play the triads.
2. Play the reference scale, saying each reference number as you play the note.
3. Play the triads again. Ask the student to sing them back in sequence notes 6-4-1 5-3-1.

Unit 2 - Midterm

I. Technic Grade ☐

A. Triads
No.(s) _____ ; key(s) _____ ; M.M. _____ ;

B. Arpeggios
No.(s) _____ ; key(s) _____ ; M.M. _____ ;

C. Drills
No.(s) _____ ; key(s) _____ ; M.M. _____ ;

D. Scales
No.(s) _____ ; key(s) _____ ; M.M. _____ ;

II. Sightreading Grade ☐   Student may study for up to 15 seconds.

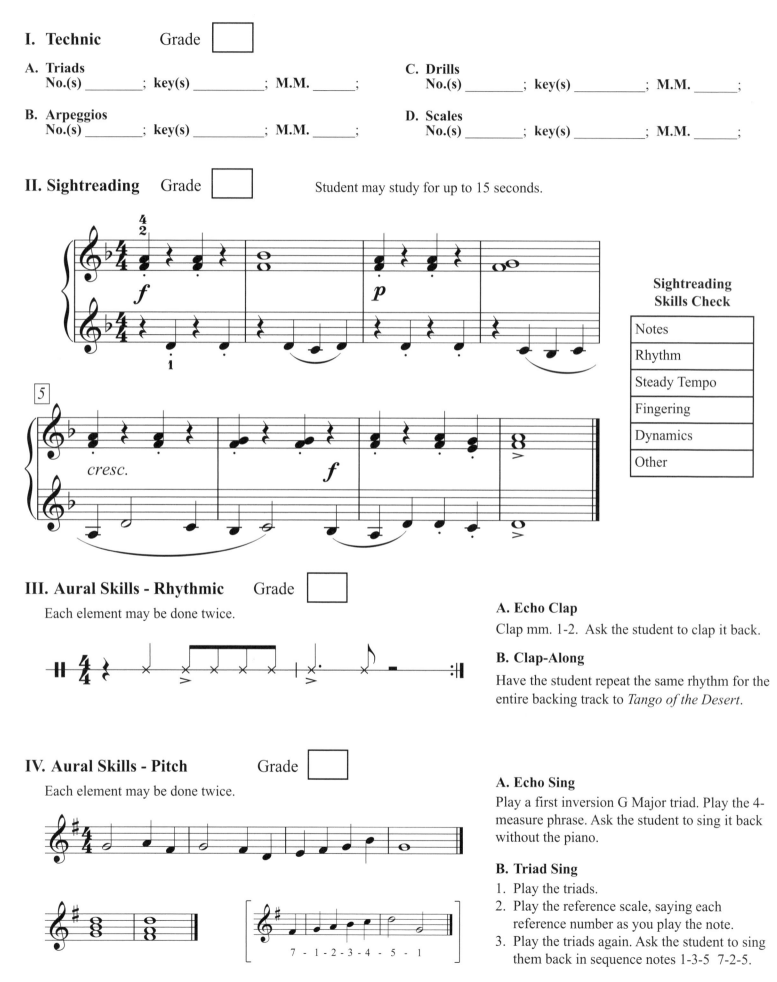

Sightreading Skills Check

| Notes |
| Rhythm |
| Steady Tempo |
| Fingering |
| Dynamics |
| Other |

III. Aural Skills - Rhythmic Grade ☐

Each element may be done twice.

A. Echo Clap

Clap mm. 1-2. Ask the student to clap it back.

B. Clap-Along

Have the student repeat the same rhythm for the entire backing track to *Tango of the Desert*.

IV. Aural Skills - Pitch Grade ☐

Each element may be done twice.

7 - 1 - 2 - 3 - 4 - 5 - 1

A. Echo Sing

Play a first inversion G Major triad. Play the 4-measure phrase. Ask the student to sing it back without the piano.

B. Triad Sing

1. Play the triads.
2. Play the reference scale, saying each reference number as you play the note.
3. Play the triads again. Ask the student to sing them back in sequence notes 1-3-5 7-2-5.

Unit 2 - Final

I. Technic   Grade ☐

A. Triads
No.(s) _____; key(s) _____; M.M. _____;

C. Drills
No.(s) _____; key(s) _____; M.M. _____;

B. Arpeggios
No.(s) _____; key(s) _____; M.M. _____;

D. Scales
No.(s) _____; key(s) _____; M.M. _____;

II. Sightreading   Grade ☐   Student may study for up to 15 seconds.

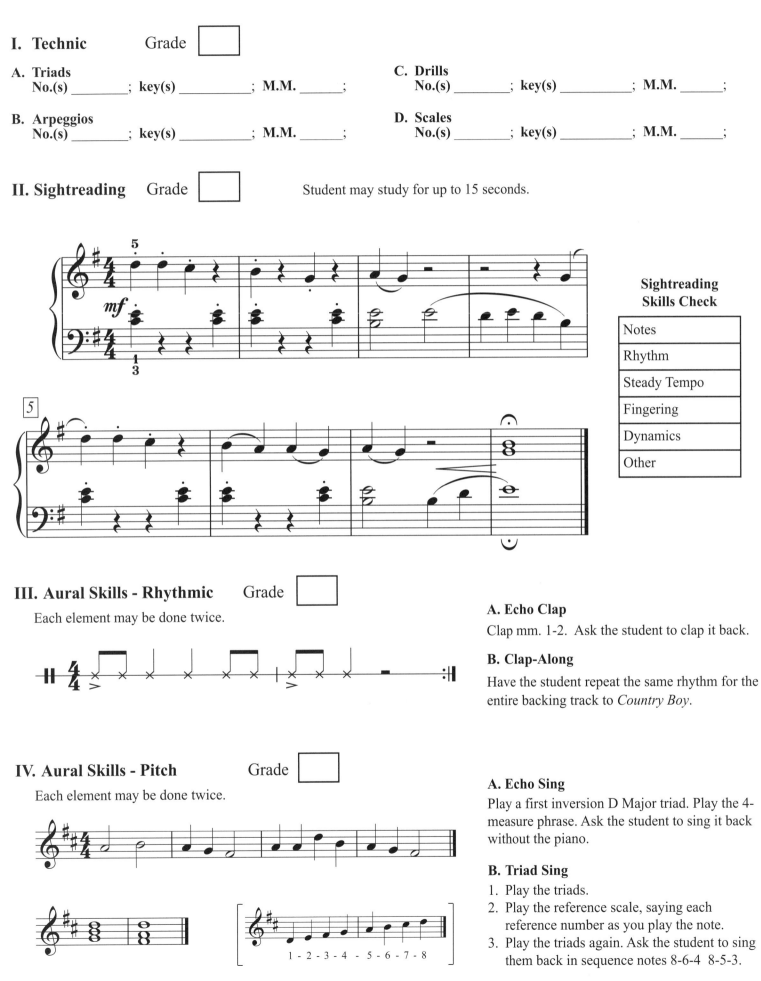

Sightreading Skills Check

Notes
Rhythm
Steady Tempo
Fingering
Dynamics
Other

III. Aural Skills - Rhythmic   Grade ☐

Each element may be done twice.

A. Echo Clap

Clap mm. 1-2. Ask the student to clap it back.

B. Clap-Along

Have the student repeat the same rhythm for the entire backing track to *Country Boy*.

IV. Aural Skills - Pitch   Grade ☐

Each element may be done twice.

A. Echo Sing

Play a first inversion D Major triad. Play the 4-measure phrase. Ask the student to sing it back without the piano.

B. Triad Sing

1. Play the triads.
2. Play the reference scale, saying each reference number as you play the note.
3. Play the triads again. Ask the student to sing them back in sequence notes 8-6-4 8-5-3.

Unit 3 - Midterm

I. Technic Grade ☐

A. Triads
No.(s) _____ ; key(s) _____ ; M.M. _____ ;

B. Arpeggios
No.(s) _____ ; key(s) _____ ; M.M. _____ ;

C. Drills
No.(s) _____ ; key(s) _____ ; M.M. _____ ;

D. Scales
No.(s) _____ ; key(s) _____ ; M.M. _____ ;

II. Sightreading Grade ☐ Student may study for up to 15 seconds.

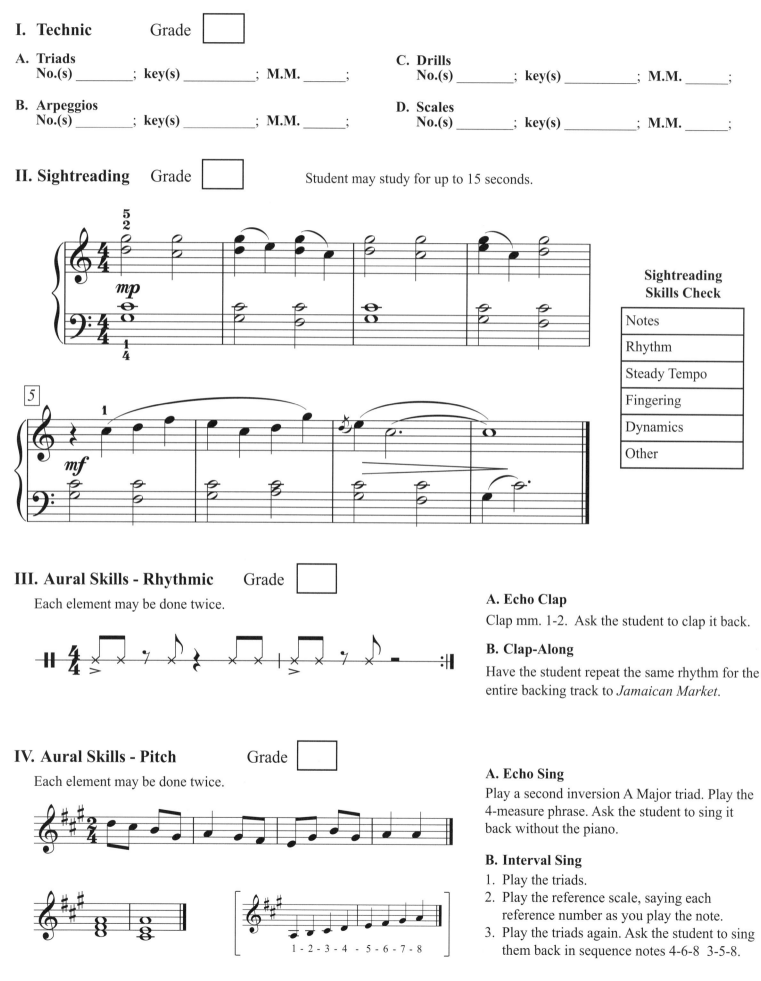

Sightreading Skills Check

| Notes |
| Rhythm |
| Steady Tempo |
| Fingering |
| Dynamics |
| Other |

III. Aural Skills - Rhythmic Grade ☐

Each element may be done twice.

A. Echo Clap

Clap mm. 1-2. Ask the student to clap it back.

B. Clap-Along

Have the student repeat the same rhythm for the entire backing track to *Jamaican Market*.

IV. Aural Skills - Pitch Grade ☐

Each element may be done twice.

1 - 2 - 3 - 4 - 5 - 6 - 7 - 8

A. Echo Sing

Play a second inversion A Major triad. Play the 4-measure phrase. Ask the student to sing it back without the piano.

B. Interval Sing

1. Play the triads.
2. Play the reference scale, saying each reference number as you play the note.
3. Play the triads again. Ask the student to sing them back in sequence notes 4-6-8 3-5-8.

Unit 3 - Final

I. Technic　　Grade ☐

A. Triads
No.(s) _____ ; key(s) _____ ; **M.M.** _____ ;

B. Arpeggios
No.(s) _____ ; key(s) _____ ; **M.M.** _____ ;

C. Drills
No.(s) _____ ; key(s) _____ ; **M.M.** _____ ;

D. Scales
No.(s) _____ ; key(s) _____ ; **M.M.** _____ ;

II. Sightreading　　Grade ☐　　Student may study for up to 15 seconds.

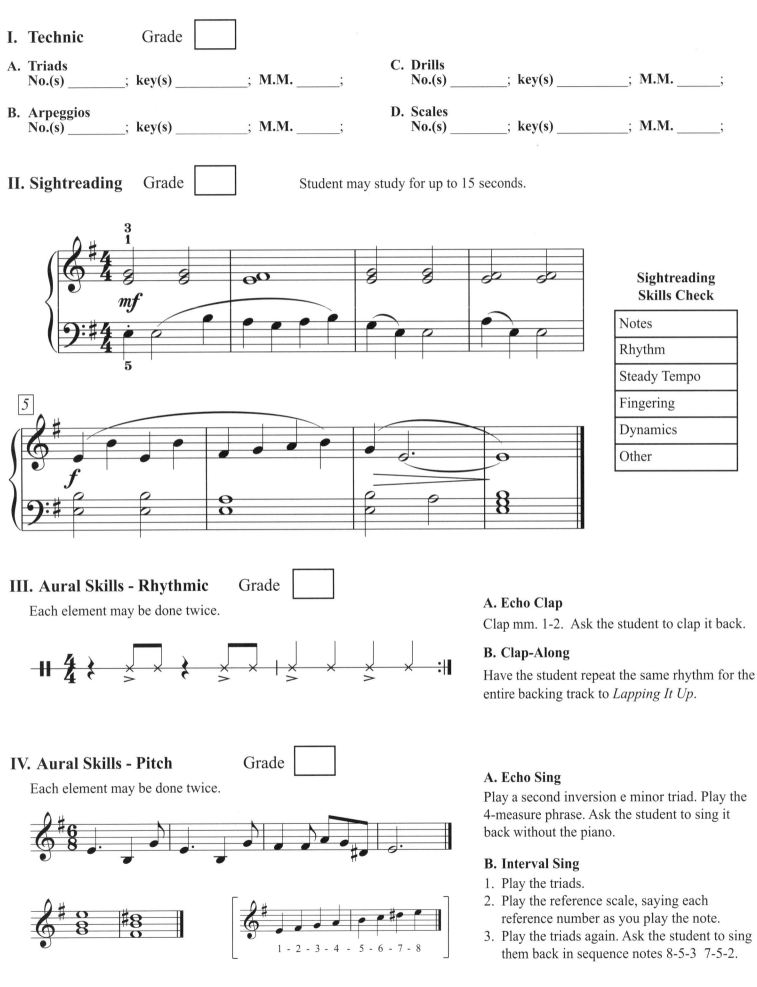

Sightreading Skills Check

| Notes |
| Rhythm |
| Steady Tempo |
| Fingering |
| Dynamics |
| Other |

III. Aural Skills - Rhythmic　　Grade ☐

Each element may be done twice.

A. Echo Clap
Clap mm. 1-2. Ask the student to clap it back.

B. Clap-Along
Have the student repeat the same rhythm for the entire backing track to *Lapping It Up*.

IV. Aural Skills - Pitch　　Grade ☐

Each element may be done twice.

A. Echo Sing
Play a second inversion e minor triad. Play the 4-measure phrase. Ask the student to sing it back without the piano.

B. Interval Sing
1. Play the triads.
2. Play the reference scale, saying each reference number as you play the note.
3. Play the triads again. Ask the student to sing them back in sequence notes 8-5-3 7-5-2.

Unit 4 - Midterm

I. Technic Grade ☐

A. Triads
No.(s) _____ ; key(s) _____ ; M.M. _____ ;

B. Arpeggios
No.(s) _____ ; key(s) _____ ; M.M. _____ ;

C. Drills
No.(s) _____ ; key(s) _____ ; M.M. _____ ;

D. Scales
No.(s) _____ ; key(s) _____ ; M.M. _____ ;

II. Sightreading Grade ☐   Student may study for up to 15 seconds.

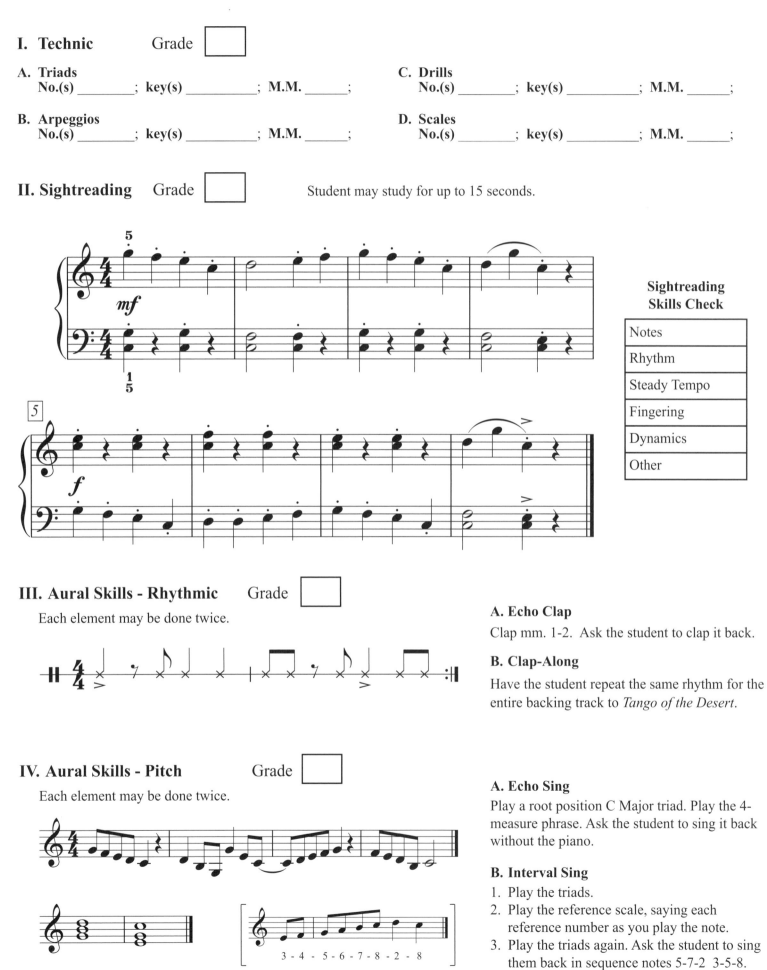

Sightreading Skills Check

Notes
Rhythm
Steady Tempo
Fingering
Dynamics
Other

III. Aural Skills - Rhythmic Grade ☐

Each element may be done twice.

A. Echo Clap

Clap mm. 1-2. Ask the student to clap it back.

B. Clap-Along

Have the student repeat the same rhythm for the entire backing track to *Tango of the Desert*.

IV. Aural Skills - Pitch Grade ☐

Each element may be done twice.

A. Echo Sing

Play a root position C Major triad. Play the 4-measure phrase. Ask the student to sing it back without the piano.

B. Interval Sing

1. Play the triads.
2. Play the reference scale, saying each reference number as you play the note.
3. Play the triads again. Ask the student to sing them back in sequence notes 5-7-2 3-5-8.

3 - 4 - 5 - 6 - 7 - 8 - 2 - 8

Unit 4 - Final

I. Technic   Grade ☐

A. Triads
No.(s) _____ ; key(s) _____ ; M.M. _____ ;

B. Arpeggios
No.(s) _____ ; key(s) _____ ; M.M. _____ ;

C. Drills
No.(s) _____ ; key(s) _____ ; M.M. _____ ;

D. Scales
No.(s) _____ ; key(s) _____ ; M.M. _____ ;

II. Sightreading   Grade ☐   Student may study for up to 15 seconds.

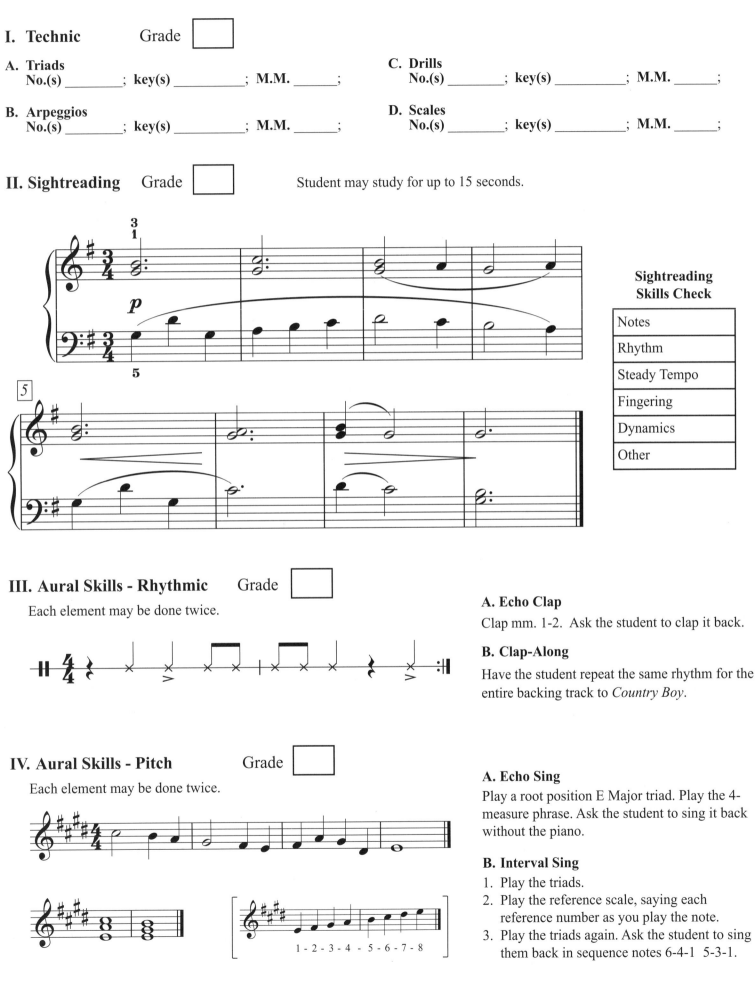

Sightreading Skills Check

| Notes |
| Rhythm |
| Steady Tempo |
| Fingering |
| Dynamics |
| Other |

III. Aural Skills - Rhythmic   Grade ☐

Each element may be done twice.

A. Echo Clap

Clap mm. 1-2. Ask the student to clap it back.

B. Clap-Along

Have the student repeat the same rhythm for the entire backing track to *Country Boy*.

IV. Aural Skills - Pitch   Grade ☐

Each element may be done twice.

1 - 2 - 3 - 4 - 5 - 6 - 7 - 8

A. Echo Sing

Play a root position E Major triad. Play the 4-measure phrase. Ask the student to sing it back without the piano.

B. Interval Sing

1. Play the triads.
2. Play the reference scale, saying each reference number as you play the note.
3. Play the triads again. Ask the student to sing them back in sequence notes 6-4-1 5-3-1.

Level 3 Scales

Basic Patterns

No. 1

No. 2

No. 3

No. 4

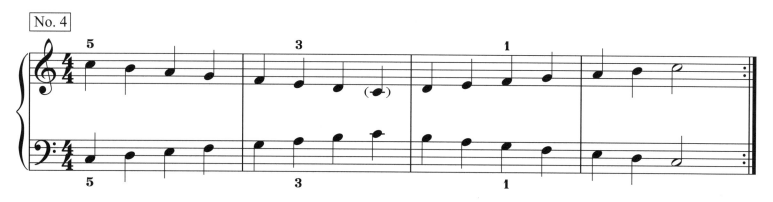

Complementary Patterns

No. 5

No. 6

No. 7

No. 8

Level 3 Triads

Cadences

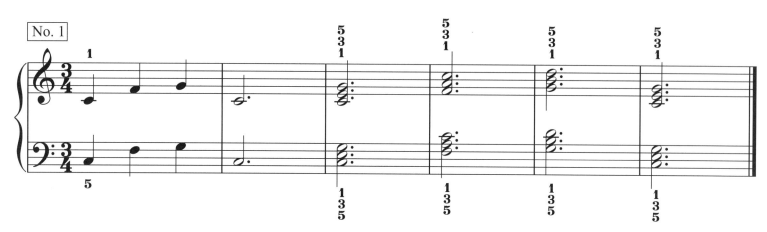

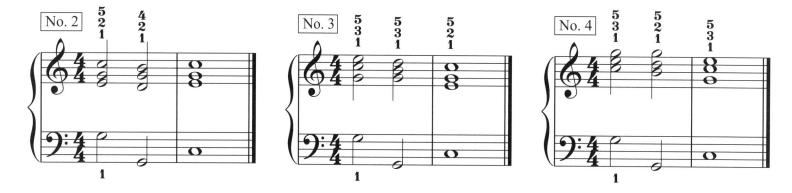

Triad Scales

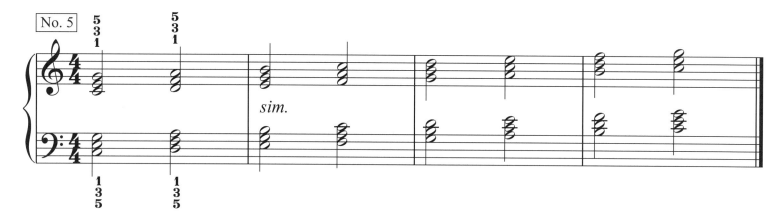

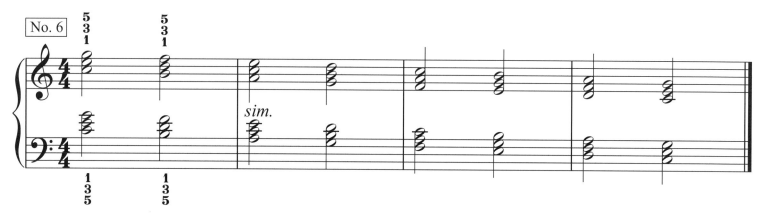

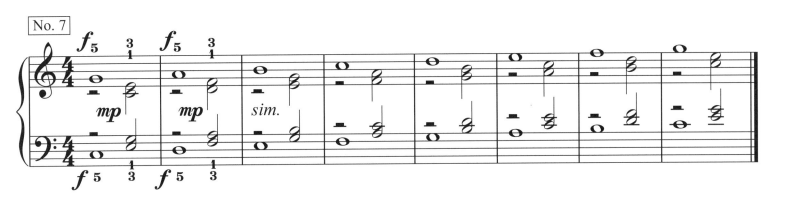

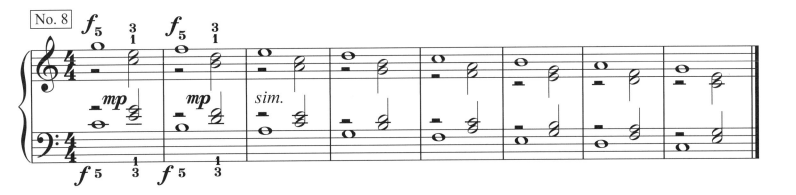

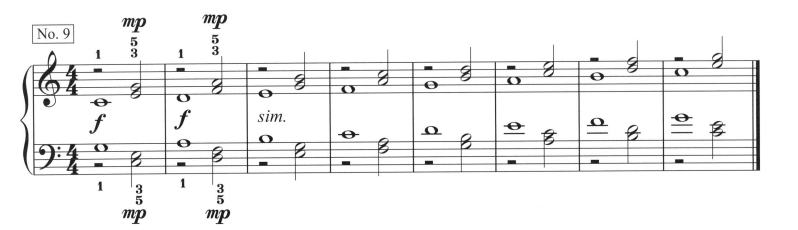

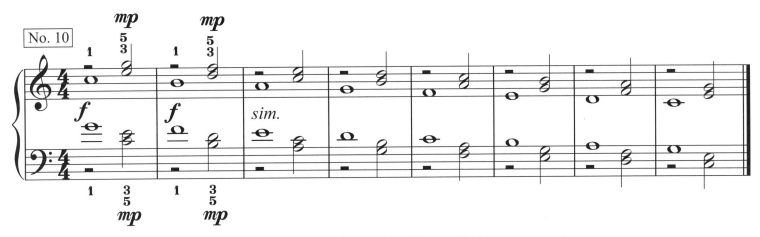

Level 3 Arpeggios

No. 1

No. 2

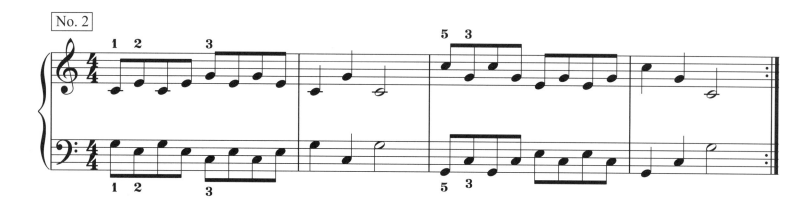

No. 3

No. 4

47

No. 5

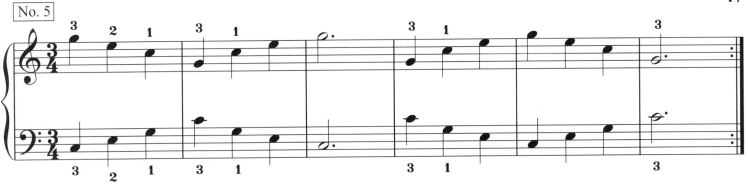

No. 6

No. 7

No. 8

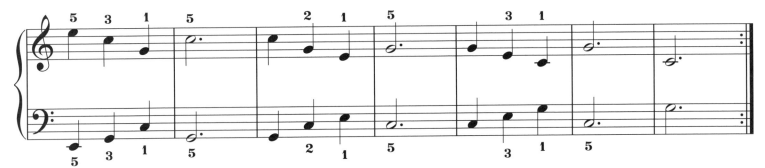

Level 3 Drills

Arm Weight Exercises

a) Rest one arm on top of your other arm.
b) Experiment with making the top arm heavy, then light. Do this by letting the arm relax down with its own weight, not by pushing.

c) Rest your third finger on the surface of the key. Play each note by gently "releasing" your arm weight into the key as you did in step b). Your wrist should not move below the level of the key.

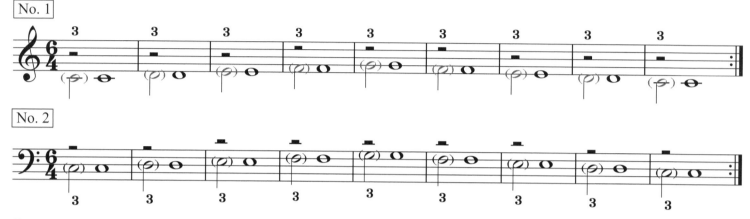

One-Note Drawbridge Exercises

a) Lift your arm about 6 inches above the key without bending at the wrist – as if it were a drawbridge. Flex your third finger so it feels strong.

b) Play each note by dropping your third finger into the key, releasing your arm weight with energy. Your wrist should not drop below key level.

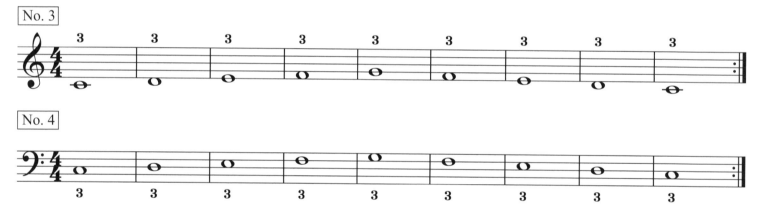

Open-Fifth Drawbridge Exercises

a) Lift your arm about 8 inches above the key without bending at the wrist – as if it were a drawbridge. Flex your thumb and fifth fingers so they feel strong.

b) Play each fifth by dropping your fingers into the keys,

releasing your arm weight with energy. Your wrist should not drop below key level.

c) Repeat steps a) & b), but this time lift your arm about 4 inches above the keys.

d) Repeat steps a) & b) lifting only 1 inch above the keys.

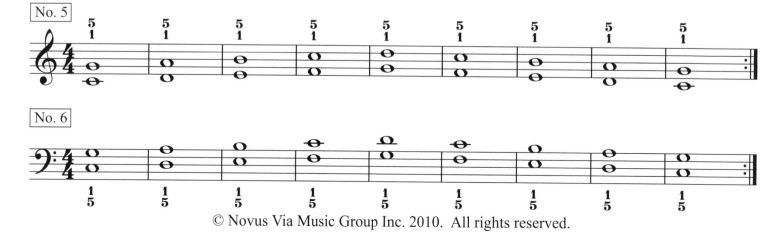

Beginning Rotation Exercises – Inward

a) Place your hand on the keys, fingers covering the five notes of the pentascale, with a good hand position.

b) Pretend you are getting ready to open a door. Rotate your hand inward, towards your thumb. The rotation motion should play the first note.

Observe that:

i) Your thumb will turn to be resting slightly on its nail.
ii) Your elbow will move slightly away from your body.
iii) The other fingers will raise above the keys.

c) Play the second note by rotating the other direction, back into position.

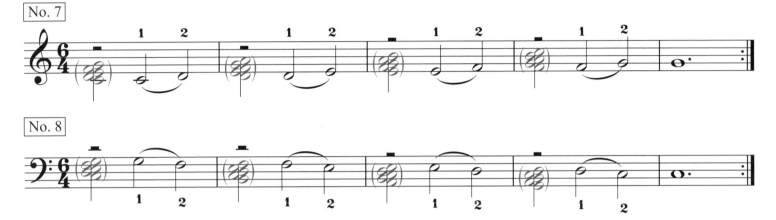

No. 7

No. 8

Beginning Rotation Exercises – Outward

a) Place your hand on the keys, fingers covering the five notes of the pentascale, with a good hand position.

b) Pretend you are getting ready to open a door. Rotate your hand outward, towards your 5th finger. The rotation motion should play the first note.

Observe that:

i) Your third finger will turn slightly onto its nail.
ii) Your elbow will move slightly in to your body.
iii) The thumb and second fingers will raise off the keys.

c) Play the second note by rotating the other direction, back into position.

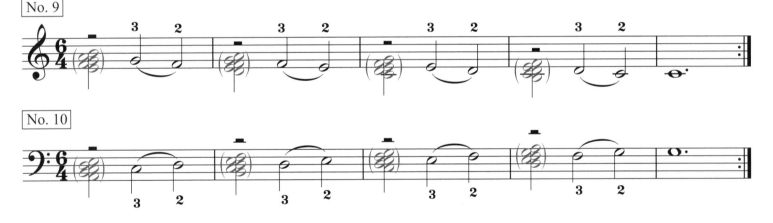

No. 9

No. 10

Fingering Variations

When you are able to play Drill nos. 7-10 with a fluid, even motion, move on to these variations which use different fingerings. Work through these before moving on to a new key.

No. 11

No. 12

No. 13

No. 14

How to Use This Book

The *American Popular Piano Skills* books are designed to be used as a flexible tool for learning the fundamental skills of playing the piano. Research tells us that the most effective way to learn is in small increments, repeated frequently. That's a good thing, considering that many piano students today have very busy schedules and may not have big chunks of time to devote to practice at one time.

How much time should you spend on basic skills? The best choice, of course, is to spend a moderate amount of time daily on technic, sightreading and ear training. But even a smaller amount of time each day, every day is better than spending a lot of time on one day after several days of non-practice.

The Open Plan System

The Open Plan organization of the *American Popular Piano Skills* books encourages skill acquisition at each student's natural pace. Review the chart below to help understand how it works.

How should you schedule assignments of Skills? Progress will vary depending on each student's needs and practice timetable.

- **Faster moving students** can do one module per week.
- **Many students** will work on two or three skill areas within a module each week.
- **Students with less practice time** often do just one skill area.

Areas that need extra work may of course be repeated as necessary.

Some Basic Tips

Singing Vocalizing has not always been part of traditional piano lessons. Yet recent research has clearly established its importance for developing crucial listening and audiating skills.

Teaching and learning singing in this context is not hard, but does take patience. Many students have not sung and will need some time and work in order to get comfortable. Stick with it! Studies have shown that even those who seem totally tone-deaf on the first attempt can improve significantly with practice.

- Check that posture is good, breathing deep and even, and throat relaxed.
- If the student is having trouble matching pitch, ask them to sing a note and hold it. Find the same pitch and sing it with them. Then ask them to move their voice with you as you sing to the correct pitch.
- Visual and verbal feedback is crucial. Saying "higher" or "lower", or moving your hand up or down to help them find the pitch is a great help.

Technic Technic should be practiced daily. Vary the focus of each week's assignment using the Technic Box in each Module.

- **Fill in the blanks** for the metronome marking (M.M.) and the number of the exercise.
- **Circle** the chosen key(s), articulation(s), and dynamic(s).

Technical exercises are set out in C Major in the last few pages of this book. For students who work better from a printed page, consider using the *Level 3 Technic Book* for the other keys.

Sightreading The word "sightreading" is a misnomer; a better term might be "pattern recognition" or even "flash learning". A good sightreader recognizes familiar patterns in new arrangements; he or she is able to think ahead, keep going despite mistakes, and keep a steady beat.

Here are some steps that have helped my students improve their sightreading:

- Play the piece at a slow tempo without stopping. After finishing, go back and circle mistakes. This builds both analysis and musical memory skills.
- Play slowly again and try to fix all the mistakes – and not add any new ones!
- Play a third time, counting out loud. This time it should be error free.

Steps may be repeated as necessary.

Mix Do you have to do all the activities for every section? You'll make the right decision based on available time, skill level and long-term goals. Remember, the most important factor in improving fundamentals is: **work on them — and do it often!!**

American Popular Piano Skills Book-Level Three

Four Learning Units		Four Examination Units	
to be done by the student at home		to be administered by the teacher at the lesson	
Each Unit contains:		Each Unit contains:	
4 Learning Modules Each module covers the following skill areas:		**2 Tests** **Midterm:** to be completed after Module 2 **Final:** to be completed after Module 4	
Technic	Triads, arpeggios, drills, and scales; along with rhythmic, dynamic, and articulation variants	**Technic**	Triads Arpeggios Drills Scales
Prepared Sightreading	A short musical excerpt	**Sightreading**	Short examples, with skills checklist
Aural Skills– Rhythmic	Metrical clapping with the backing track, written work	**Aural Skills– Rhythmic**	Echo Clap Clap-Along
Aural Skills– Pitch	Triad sing, sing-along, written work	**Aural Skills– Pitch**	Echo Sing Triad Sing